Carrie and Company

CARRIER AND COMPANY
POSITIVELY CHIC INTERIORS

JESSE CARRIER AND MARA MILLER

WITH
JUDITH NASATIR

FOREWORD BY
ANNA WINTOUR

———

THE VENDOME PRESS
NEW YORK

CONTENTS

FOREWORD

That Jesse Carrier should have chosen to work in a world in which chairs feature so prominently doesn't surprise me one bit. After all, what profession besides interior decorator relies on chairs as much as therapist or counselor? In his working life, Jesse manages to be both of those—as well as a decorating genius. When collaborating with him, as I have done rather often, what I've found most striking is that the process leading to the end result—a place you will love, and which you can live in unselfconsciously—is always an incredibly calm and reassuring experience.

Most recently, I asked Jesse to help put the finishing touches on the decoration of my country house for the wedding of my son, Charlie. (He'd already designed the interiors, which you can see on pages 17–25 and 85–101.) There were, of course, a million and one strongly expressed opinions as to how everything should look. My enduring memory of the preparations is of Jesse solicitously listening to every thought and comment, quietly nodding as he scribbled them down in his notebook—and then, miraculously, somehow managing to please everyone.

The act of pleasing a client is something that Jesse and Mara Miller, his wonderful partner in life and work, do on a daily basis, and they do so by recognizing that how we live is not always meant to be picture-ready. "Life does not have to be perfect. Furnishings and possessions do not have to be perfect," they state in one of the essays that accompany the many beautiful interiors in this book.

As I looked through the pages, that philosophy of decorating was entirely evident. I wasn't taken just by the elegance and exactitude of the aesthetic decisions, the flawless mix of neoclassicist rigor and Scandinavian chic, the Art Deco élan and the rustic simplicity, but by how each and every interior here embodies a real sense of personal charm; these are homes whose high style comes from a very human-scaled sense of warmth and joy. But when one considers they are the work of Jesse and Mara, that's exactly to be expected.

—Anna Wintour

INTRODUCTION

At Carrier and Company, we love interiors with atmosphere and personality. We want the homes that we design to have breathing room, a certain dreaminess, and strength of character. We prize decoration that feels effortless, essential, and light of spirit. It is that open, airy quality that we believe gives our rooms life. Yet we are dedicated to creating the firm foundations of functional beauty that are necessary in order to live with ease, style, and comfort. That is the passionate discipline and disciplined passion of our approach to design: we are truly comfortable with less, yet we are open to all possibilities.

Professional partnerships are unusual in our line of work, which prizes a singular vision above all. But in our decade of professional union, Mara and I have discovered that we often have the same design instincts—that we are a dichotomy working toward a single purpose. Perhaps that is because we had a domestic partnership before we began our professional bond, and so had intimate experience of the sparks of inspiration and insight that come from our two interacting points of view as well as a shared vision for how much better, more interesting, more creative two can be than one.

What we learned in the ten years that we each worked for other masterly designers before joining forces informs the logic, purpose, and sensibility of every choice that now we make together. From Thomas O'Brien, I absorbed much about interpreting America's historic vernaculars for modern lifestyles, and the enormous refinement necessary to create simplicity. From Jeffrey Bilhuber, I gained a deeper understanding of the melting-pot nature of our American design heritage, how to transform the pretty into the practical and the practical into the pretty in rooms, and how to translate big ideas into beautiful, comfortable realities.

While Jesse comes at design versed in bold, American perspectives, my training has given me a more Continental or eclectic point of view. At Sills Huniford Associates, I fell for Stephen and Ford's aesthetic of unique daring, refinement, and ethereality. From Marcy V. Masterson,

I absorbed the tangible translation of perfection and quality. With Sara Bengur, I gained insight into the global magic of color and pattern.

A decade into our careers, after the birth of our first child, it became clear that to make our family work best, we needed to partner rather than divide and conquer. And so, with Jack, Carrier and Company was born!

As you will see in the following pages, we delight in working across the spectrum of interior styles, from bohemian glamour to country charm, from modern luxe to the timeless and ineffable, and from the historically informed to the tailored and refined. We make our selections based on what is appropriate to a project's architecture and geographic context, and to the client's preferences, identity, and taste. Because each of us understands these ideas in our own way, we use that creative tension to find the balance of practicality, personality, and presence that is positively chic, and that we seek in the interiors we design at Carrier and Company.

PRECEDING PAGE The family portrait, a gift from Annie Leibovitz, was taken by her for the Corcoran "Live Who You Are" campaign; it features us with our two children, Jack and Natalie, in our New York City apartment. **OPPOSITE** The reception area of our office at Carrier and Company, a light-filled loft in New York City, always contains a rotating mix of treasures, finds, and client pieces.

TIMELESSNESS

We think that when it comes to design and decorating, timelessness is the love child of modern and traditional. Like our modern interiors, our timeless rooms embrace—and celebrate—visual crispness and clarity. Yet they meld that cleanness and precision with the hues, the familiar forms, and the rich textures that speak of tradition. And by definition, they eschew the trendy.

In projects where timelessness is the desired outcome, we selectively mix references to the past, the present, and the future. Antiques are obviously important to the equation. A piece or two from the mid-twentieth century will lighten any weight of history that antiques bring with them and usher the mix into the present. Folding in something surprising, perhaps something totally of the moment, then gives the room an up-to-the-minute accent. Yet when we choose those pieces from the now, we consciously avoid anything that we think will shout too loudly of today in the days to come.

For us, decorating is always all about the mix. A room's style—a home's style—derives from the pairings, the compositions, the accents and details. Unexpected choices in scale, material, or placement, a daring use of bold color or finish, may arrest the eye and stop time.

It is possible to imbue a more traditional interior with a modern sensibility, and vice versa. Take a classic eighteenth-century French chair—or an American Windsor, a banister-back, a Chippendale ball-and-claw foot, or a Sheraton sofa, for that matter. These are intrinsic to our heritage, and we understand how their creators meant them to look, feel, and be. Yet when they surprise us, as they sometimes do, with a stripped or lacquered frame, they feel more of our time than of their own period.

Even if every piece in a room happens to be pretty, or vintage, or charming, or traditional, it is possible to arrange these components in such a way as to capture the eye and pique the imagination. The marriage of blue and white, for example, is arguably the most enduring love

match in decorating—and as traditional a union as exists in our domestic visual vocabulary. But even as classic as blue and white is—and it is as classic, and beloved, as it gets—it can be as modern as tomorrow depending on its use. Deployed with daring, placed in an unusual context, it delights and surprises.

The unpredictable is never traditional. The mix that defies expectations—that includes an indefinable something that renders it new—ultimately makes a room more vibrant in spirit and endows it with the ability to age. Editing is essential to the effect, especially with traditional décor: paring down truly classic elements to their absolute essence, without ornament, seems to us to lighten the weight of history, to make the pieces and their combination fresh, youthful, and lasting, to ensure that the mix won't appear dated anytime soon, and that it will age beautifully.

Steadfast longevity is our aim as designers, because we want our clients to enjoy their residences time and time again, and hopefully years from now. Rooms that are timeless, elegant, and chic withstand the tests of time not because they are outside of time but because they manage to survey time—to look forward and backward through the history of design, decoration, and style.

PAGE 17 In a sunny corner of this country house, white enameled floors, formal curtains in a contemporary fabric, and an industrial light fixture make for an ageless mix—and a great place for gaming. **PRECEDING PAGES** Dressing up the living room are traditional upholstery forms, Swedish pieces, and wall paneling. Rustic touches—sea grass on the floor, antique lounge chairs covered in vintage blue-and-white grain sacks, and a bricklayer's table for a coffee table—relieve the formality. **ABOVE** Elliott Puckette's painting above the fireplace adds a pop of modernity. **OPPOSITE** Colorful nineteenth-century French pottery on the coffee table and pillows dressed in vintage textiles disarm with casual charm.

ABOVE Playing with scale is one way to bring an old house completely up-to-date. On the upstairs landing, Hugo Guinness's towering painting of tall-stemmed flowers seems to dwarf the already diminutive Swedish painted chest of drawers. **OPPOSITE** Symmetry and pairings allow rustic objects such as these Swedish painted-and-gilded mirrors and candlestick lamps to feel more formal, especially when grouped with a true country piece like this scrub pine trestle table. The knots of the pine wall paneling bleed through the whitewash finish, creating a very subtle freeform, almost modern pattern.

OPPOSITE AND ABOVE A tray ceiling carved out of an attic space overhead gives this bedroom height and drama. The washed knotty pine continues the theme of the upstairs landing, seen on the preceding pages. An odd Asian painted cupboard, the client's own Swedish Deco chairs, a Bennison print hanging airily at the windows, and a bed that's a contemporary take on a French campaign style add up to what we think is a classic, characterful English country house mix.

PRECEDING PAGES For this home in the Hamptons, the client's directive was explicit: "Create a new version of an old American house." We thought there was no better way to do that than by honoring—and updating—the tradition of blue and white. As for the chandelier, it's French 1940s, found by the client in Paris. **ABOVE** This window seat gave us the opportunity to create an intimate area within a formal space for curling up and getting cozy. **OPPOSITE** A plain, rusticated, burlaplike material on the Swedish daybed feels unexpected and relaxed in this comparatively formal room. **OVERLEAF** In the dining room, cushioned and upholstered walls with en suite curtain fabric play up the contrast between the décor's rustic and refined elements.

ABOVE AND OPPOSITE At the center of the dining room is a weathered, zinc-topped Belgian-style table on a rusticated base, which adds an indoor-outdoor sensibility that makes sense in a room that opens to the garden. Dining chairs are upholstered for maximum comfort. Cobalt stemware and vases, napkins, and arrangements of garden flowers continue the blue-and-white theme.

A MASTERFUL MIX

For many years, one of decorating's dominant aesthetics favored interiors that were collected and uniform. Residences were done entirely in Biedermeier or Art Deco, eighteenth-century French or Shaker style, and so on. Then, as inevitably happens, that particular attitude about style shifted in tone from the match to the mix. It became increasingly acceptable to co-mingle styles and periods in one room. As young designers, that stimulated us. We realized that if we kept aspects of design in concert—proportion, scale, or formality, for example—we could combine disparate pieces in such a way that each helped the others express themselves and show off their best features.

By and large, our clients come to us with the oddments of their lives so far—pieces from both spouses that they want us to honor and use. This is natural in the blending of marriages, and of families. To meld these individual points of view, we will often edit the possessions yet broaden the existing mix to create visual bridges. We will paper the walls with a contemporary print, on top of which we'll hang the client's historic maps and favorite photographs. We'll pair a tight-back, skirted sofa with a rolled arm—a classic modern upholstery form—with a Chippendale armchair and a brass drum-top table pulled up close by to set a drink, a contemporary coffee table with a rush top that is newly made but handcrafted, a mid-1950s Italian brass torchère, and a hand-woven wool rug. The individual components do not share a heritage or an aesthetic, but visually they harmonize beautifully. Finding just the right couplings, adjacencies, and balance is an organic process—and much of it is unconscious.

As our eye gets better and better trained, our understanding of the mix evolves. Our ideal is the perfectly imperfect. In synthesized rooms that are precise to the point of perfection, one wrong note can be incredibly disruptive. The mix is very forgiving. Life does not have to be perfect. Furnishings and possessions do not have to be perfect. But you can still live beautifully.

OPPOSITE In this Hamptons sitting room, a wallpaper with a watercolorlike pattern creates an unusual backdrop for a mix of disparate forms, textures, and materials unified through color and artisanal quality. The antique armchair is upholstered in a hand-woven Tara Chapas textile, and the wool rug was hand woven in Guatemala. In contrast are the highly polished mid-century brass drum table and torchère. **OVERLEAF** The maps on the wall allude to the view of the ocean outside the window. Mahogany paneled doors honor the house's architecture, which takes its cues from the nineteenth-century Shingle Style vernacular of Long Island.

OPPOSITE In a classic mid-century glass box, the furnishings marry Continental family heirlooms to more modern possessions. A painted twentieth-century French-style desk serves as a dressing table. ABOVE Talk about strange bedfellows. In the same master bedroom, a scenic screen pairs unexpectedly with the mid-century-inspired artwork and furnishings.

ABOVE In a glamorous Palm Beach–style Florida bedroom, damask hand-blocked bed hangings that match the curtains establish the bed as a cohesive, elegant retreat within a large, vaulted space. **OPPOSITE** Underfoot is an incredibly luxurious plush carpet with a surprising modern pinstripe. A faux-rattan chair pulls up to the French Deco table, where a Murano bedside lamp adds shimmer in more ways than one.

ABOVE AND RIGHT In the same bedroom, a sitting area contains an unexpected mix of materials. The faceted mirror table brings a touch of the now to an otherwise timeless collection of furnishings. The settee is a 1930s piece recovered in crosshatched silver-blue cotton velvet from Rogers & Goffigon; satin pillows and the twin shagreen-wrapped tables dyed shades of celadon contribute elements of sheen.

TAILORED REFINEMENT

Traditional design is foundational to each of our projects, regardless of that project's particular style. As paradoxical as that may seem, it is anything but. Our regard for the classic formulations of design and decoration comes largely from our education. It has grounded us in the history of the decorative arts and the style continuum of architecture and ornament. We are trained in the practical techniques that teach the eye to see and know proper form, proportion, scale, elevation, plan, and composition. For us, traditional design is like figurative drawing for art students: *the* essential visual language that must be learned, absorbed, and mastered before graduating to abstraction and beyond.

What does any of this have to do with what we're calling "tailored refinement"? Everything. Design involves relationships and adjustments by increments. In our design process, we both defer and refer to tradition. We use it as the core, then tip away from it into other styles—modern, tailored, timeless, country, and so on—to suit the individual client and the specific context of the residence. The way we go through this process defines who we are as designers.

Styles do progress, and the line between them can be very fine. One look may vary from another by mere degrees. Tailored rooms, for example, are akin to modern rooms: they are clean and pared down, but refined in such a way that they feel a little more sensual, a little more lush, a little more plush. Their geometry speaks clearly, but it does so with a softer, gentler, though still precise edge. Tailored rooms may be traditional as well. Whether a tailored room swings toward tradition or toward the modern depends on the balance of its components. But what makes the style tailored as opposed to, say, country or bohemian? It is the focus and the logic that we apply to the editing process. The desired goal here is rooms that are urbane and sophisticated, yet comfortable and welcoming too.

Our tailored rooms by definition avoid frivolous decorative embellishments, yet they embrace considerable visual play and the presence of strong patterns. They also, perhaps surprisingly, incorporate a great deal of detail. What they lack is the distraction of look-at-me ornamentation—in other words, no swags, ruffles, or rosettes. The niceties of the curtains are as definitive as good grammar: clean, smart, and understated. Any upholstery details are unobtrusive enhancements, as are those of the lampshades. There may well be simple little trims, but those simple little trims always have a very definite purpose: they clarify and define, they finish. Such discreet touches give all sorts of forms the advantage of crispness, clarity, and refined detail. For us, such quiet statements and understated flourishes bespeak a certain glamour.

Rather like the most classic suiting materials, the palettes of these rooms tend to the monochromatic. In the same way, they frequently encompass the element of a compelling graphic pattern. Accents include the merest whisper of gleam, and occasional strokes of color. For us, this tailored approach honors the beauty of restraint, the pleasure in the perfect fit, and the appreciation of subdued polish.

PAGE 45 Two antique Oushaks and a pair of potted figs relax the grandeur of this long Florida entry hall; contemporary plaster sand-dollar-inspired light fixtures by Marc Bankowsky and a giant clamshell atop a Dunbar chest introduce local references. PRECEDING PAGES In the living room, a polished spoon-back chair and carved Jansen-style sofa speak of formality, echoing that of the doorways' arched trim molding. The custom flat-woven sisal carpet, the broad horizontal stripes of the club chair upholstery, and modern batik-printed throw pillows lighten the effect, while fine piping on the lampshades and nailhead trim on the chairs bridge the two moods with tailored details. ABOVE This French 1930s Art Deco coffee table has the most glamorous zebrawood marquetry. OPPOSITE Enhancing the room's material mix is a pair of 1970s tables with marbleized-lacquer tops and simple gilt-bronze bases. OVERLEAF Pops of lemon zest and marigold inject sunshine into the neutral palette; basic white walls are made special with a polished-plaster finish.

THE ART OF PLACEMENT

In every project, we consider and reconsider how to resolve the countless questions that come up as we're working our way toward visual harmony. In essence, those many questions generally boil down to some variation on these two: What goes where? And does that go there? That is the art of placement, and it matters to us very much. With artful placement—prominent siting, unexpected orientation, a frame of negative space, dense arrangements—a designer can create significant moments out of virtually nothing. The more negative space around an object, the greater the dramatic impact and perceived significance. Density also changes the visual atmosphere, as objects appear cozier in clusters. Further, the client's personality emerges based on a tolerance for the type and concentration of the room's contents.

The designer's use of shapes and forms can successfully transform the utilitarian necessity of the furniture plan into something much more artful. Scale, shape, and balance contribute to the effect. Beyond functionality, every room is about its vistas, about what the eye sees from each vantage point. We think about where we want visual weight, visual quiet, how and where and what will draw focus. The same holds true for an enfilade of rooms, where we use scale and depth, height and breadth, to introduce a perceptible, visible, spatial rhythm that enhances the flow from one room to the next.

We strive to place objects in unexpected, impactful positions. When arrangements are too well balanced, they may grow flat, even boring. An oddball piece of furniture of an unexpected scale, style, or provenance can—and often does—make the overall room more exciting.

We work to make each individual element become part of the room—not apart from the room. We never want one work of art to be competitive or one piece of furniture to be a scene-stealer. At the end of the day, everything in a room has to comingle, to play nicely together—even, occasionally, to flirt. If one component, such as a wall-sized photograph or painting, becomes too demanding, we may veil it with other pieces to redirect the eye. We want our clients and their family and friends to appreciate each room—and each residence—in its entirety.

OPPOSITE The organic and the polished play out in this remarkable, unexpected, site-specific artwork, which energizes the space around it. Artist Ran Adler conceived and created the spiral work for this location, and then installed it, weaving reeds and river grass with wire and fixing the elements piece by piece to the wall with thorns.

ABOVE AND RIGHT This is a case of life imitating art. Actual melons and amaryllis blossoms atop the formal, French-polished antique French dining table mirror the painting above the batik-linen-wrapped Karl Springer console table. Wall brackets of coral suggest context; the birds, a touch of whimsy. A Colonial brass chandelier dipped in white plaster feels modern here.

LEFT In this guest bedroom, playful horizontally striped wallpaper further energizes the bright green of the plush velvet that we used in strong silhouettes. The unexpected watercolorlike striping simultaneously softens and modernizes the room. Paler and earthier shades of green in the custom bedding quiet the high contrast of the scheme. **ABOVE** In a mid-century-inspired vignette, a Tommi Parzinger desk serves double duty as a vanity table. The slim, blackened-steel-and-brass chair is French 1940s, and the Lucite-and-brass-framed mirror is vintage 1970s.

LEFT The family room, which opens onto a lanai, connects directly to the kitchen. Saturated color and mid-century pieces give the room a casual, family-oriented atmosphere, but the contrast cord on the sofas and French adjustable-back reclining chairs reference the glamour of a 1940s luxury liner. ABOVE The bright, happy colors of the family room carry into the kitchen. Chippendale-style bamboo seating is a familiar form made punchy in coral lacquer. The brilliant yellow encaustic-painted concrete tiles of the backsplash make for a sunny kitchen. Metal pendant shades hung with French link dress up the kitchen island. OVERLEAF LEFT For this perfect little pool cabana, which offers an intimate spot out of the sun, we custom-fabricated the inset arched mirror to enlarge the room and reflect the pool. A U-shaped built-in banquette was designed for lounging. OVERLEAF RIGHT Poolside pleasures? The reference to Slim Aarons couldn't be clearer.

PRECEDING PAGES Throughout the house, we fabricated custom curtain hardware with simple returns, rather than finials, to downplay the formality of the curtains and create a consistency from room to room. In the den, linen-wrapped walls create a cool spot for cocooning; grosgrain ribbon trimmed with nailheads covers the seams. ABOVE An Art Deco–style cut velvet dresses up this Billy Baldwin slipper chair. OPPOSITE Clearly, hanging art is part and parcel of the art of placement. Here, the gallery-style grouping of works by Joseph F. Cada, Richard Koppe, and Medard Klein— all dating from 1945 to 1949—provides a bracing, witty contrast with the tailored nature of the room.

PRECEDING PAGES In the library of a classic prewar apartment in New York, tailored architecture uses bookcases to establish symmetry. Thick, geometrically patterned jute carpet, whip-stitched cowhide poofs, and contemporary patterned pillows create low-key tribal chic. LEFT In the living room, casually placed organic forms offset the more defined geometries of the lounge chairs and rug. ABOVE The vintage glass-topped occasional table adds function without visual heaviness. OVERLEAF Contemporary street art by A.S.V.P. contributes an unexpected element, while the hand-worked pillow textiles soften the wood-and-metal-framed sofa from Holly Hunt and tailored upholstery.

PRECEDING PAGES In the dining room, built-in wine storage is concealed behind paneled cupboards. While an antique sideboard, faceted ceramic lamps, and tufted-velvet dining chairs hint at formality, the leather-bound ribbed carpet, roman shades, and contemporary staggered pendant chandeliers are modern. OPPOSITE To create striking variety with subtle tones, the secret is a mix of textures: a chair upholstered in a ribbed fabric, a gauffraged and painted velvet pillow, an ombré woven throw, and an embroidered linen curtain. ABOVE, CLOCKWISE FROM TOP LEFT Tall waterfall skirts with inverted pleats at the corners bring femininity and drama to the simple lines of the chair and ottoman; dark wood lends richness and contrast to a pale scheme; a mirrored piece of furniture makes keen sense in this understated bedroom, where quiet reflections are the norm; linen-wrapped drawers add texture to the custom dresser and visually lighten its generous size.

ABOVE The entry of a New York apartment featuring classic herringbone floors is brought up-to-date with a tribal carpet and contemporary lighting. **RIGHT** Walls covered in woven raffia, rich and saturated mohair-dressed club chairs, saddle-stitched leather cubes, and a patterned rug create a natty combination in the family room.

PRECEDING PAGES In a pied-à-terre on Central Park South, a paneled-and-mirrored wall treatment expands the incredible park views. Unlined wool challis curtains filter the light softly. **ABOVE** Polished-nickel octagonal hardware acts like jewelry on black-lacquered door panels. **OPPOSITE** In the living room, a Milo Baughman barrel-back chair from the 1970s has been cleverly upholstered to accentuate the shape of its metal base.

OPPOSITE A custom windowpane-patterned bedcover reinforces a handsome but soft aesthetic. **ABOVE** A lacquered-linen bedside chest sits perfectly within the architectural frame of the paneled mirrored wall; its texture adds patina to the room, as do the decorative glazed wall treatment and deeply tufted headboard.

COUNTRY CHARM

Some people find the word *charm* rather off-putting, especially in the context of design and decorating, and particularly as it applies to country interiors. We are not quite sure why. We like charm. As decorators, we aspire to it. We want to create alluring rooms and interiors that beguile, captivate, enrapture, enchant, mesmerize—in a word, charm. For us, this connotes decorating of a certain grace and character. Rooms in this mode do not try to be anything other than what they are. They are perfect in themselves, in their own way. This very absence of pretension is precisely what makes charm and country such natural partners in our minds.

We find that people are more willing to indulge their sense of fantasy in their country residences. The visual vocabulary that goes with these rooms allows for far more romance and whimsy than most other styles. At its core is a form of nostalgia, a belief in—or at least an eye for—the beauty of uncomplicated times and straightforward pleasures. People imagine rubber boots, apple picking in quilted jackets, horses and hayrides, or the beach equivalent of all that. They want their rooms to cater to that vision, to express that ideal, yet in an authentic way. As a result, the décor may feel caught in a moment or a memory, which is the source of the nostalgia. This can seem to slow down time, which is what the fantasy of country living is about for many.

Country rooms tend to celebrate the quality of rusticity, particularly in wall treatments and floor finishes, and often in individual pieces of furniture and fabric choices. The mix will likely include slipcovered pieces, kilim-covered pieces, twig furniture, sisal rugs, and wrought-iron railings and curtain hardware. It may extend to industrial and agricultural items salvaged from older structures nearby and repurposed for today, everything from an original soapstone parlor sink unearthed in a local barn to reclaimed wide-plank pine floors rescued from

a house or farm structure about to go under the wrecking ball. Those are the items that will help make a country room stylish and chic. They all represent a specific type of simplicity, one that can be extremely refined and sophisticated, although clearly not polished to a high gloss. There is a certain kind of plainness—an unvarnished, or at least undecorated truth—that speaks of authenticity. It resides in the inherent beauty of furnishings and objects created entirely for function and utility. Their surfaces are likely to be raw or untreated, and very often reveal the history of their use and the hands of their maker.

Country rooms that have any sort of charm at all are inevitably laid back and relaxed. Is there a gentility to the rusticity? Is that the wellspring of the charm? We cannot say for certain. What we do know is that we let these rooms be what they are, and then we embellish them with care and restraint—and when it suits, a spirit of playfulness.

PAGE 85 The conversion of this nineteenth-century barn into a guesthouse was a project in conservation. The interior frame is original, with wallboards that are actually the reverse sides of the barn's old siding. To preserve the structure's appearance, patina, and texture, we built a new exterior shell. PRECEDING PAGES Brick flooring and simple wrought-iron railings and window hardware wink at the nature of the place. Swedish, English, and Anglo-Indian pieces fit right in with its casual, rustic spirit. ABOVE A custom brass sink and bar top were oxidized to create a patina; the plumbing hardware is antique in style. RIGHT To salvage the rafters in the second-floor bedroom, we put a new roof over the old one. New wallboards line the interior.

ABOVE A nineteenth-century painting of a stallion makes a tongue-in-cheek comment in a building that was once a stable. Crewelwork bedding and a classic American hand-woven rug speak to the rustic elegance. Simple window curtains of unbleached cotton have a shoelace-style drawstring detail that feels both homespun and chic. OPPOSITE The old soapstone parlor sink in the bathroom was a forgotten relic that we found on the property and resurrected.

ABOVE One of a suite of individual guest barns and cottages, this guest place includes a comfy vintage wingback chair and ottoman; the patterned linen on the chair back and arms was original to the chair, so we kept it and replaced the cushions, now covered in a hefty hemp fabric that's close to burlap. **RIGHT** In the bedroom, reclaimed pine floors add character, as does a bench made from reclaimed lumber by Jefferson West Antiques. At the foot of the bed, a new bench is upholstered in repurposed mover's blankets. The four-poster is an American antique that we had altered to fit today's mattresses. **OVERLEAF** The library barn is a new structure married to an old one, and designed as a secluded space for study and to house the client's growing collection of reference books.

OPPOSITE In the library barn, old maps augment the learned atmosphere while offering notes of pattern and color. We were able to introduce apertures in the new portion of the structure, including doors that open to the garden and allow light to flood in. ABOVE The horse in the Steven Klein photograph hanging over the sofa seems to be gazing intently at the room. OVERLEAF A study in the main house is a private retreat imbued with an English country house feeling.

ABOVE Open doors and white-painted floors visually connect the ground-level rooms of this house to create a sense of oneness. The dining room shows the client's fascination with blue and white; the tablecloth is made from a vintage grain sack. **OPPOSITE** In the sitting room, rag-glazed paneled walls create a rustic-yet-refined background for a George Smith rolled-arm sofa covered in a Bennison print.

A CONNECTION TO HISTORY

We take our cues on what and how we blend history into a project from that project's architecture and location. This is a soft approach, and interpretive, but it has the advantage of contextual appropriateness. For those reasons, history for us tends to lean toward the vernacular. We like making a sense of place. We try always to be cognizant of the spirit and the physical facts of location—to that particular lifestyle, specific climate, and typical activities. If a client has three homes, our goal is to make sure that no one looks like the others, and that each looks and feels appropriate to where it is.

We also turn to historical precedents when the architecture of a home, for whatever reason, may not relate as well as it could to those most human of desires—our deep yearnings for emotional and physical comfort. The ability to satisfy those longings is just one reason why we find design and decoration so purposeful. And why we think history matters. If a Shingle Style house in the Hamptons either is, or is based on, a local building type, it makes ultimate good sense to use forms, materials, textures, and patterns that speak that same visual language. Old plank floors that have been cleaned and waxed, a naïve all-over floral pattern that accentuates a dormered ceiling, a ladder-back chair with a hand-woven rush seat, and candle wall sconces converted to lamp light work together in such a context to reassure with the comfort of age and history.

It is unlikely that we will ever do a period-perfect room. We may decide on a specific type of wood paneling or painted beadboard—historically informed choices—to finish walls in a house done in the style of particular region or era, but we will select that option for its decorative ends rather than its period aims. We will start from that reference point because it suits the architecture of the house, and interpret the motif freely.

We take liberties with history. And we make appropriate nods to it, where appropriate, because a house should always tell where you are in the world, and when.

OPPOSITE In this converted Hamptons guest barn, the second-floor loft, furnished with a cozy daybed, is the ultimate under-the-eaves retreat. The door opens onto a balcony that overlooks a trellis. **OVERLEAF** In the bedroom, a petite-print fabric covers the walls above the white-painted beadboard dado. Lampshades with shirred pleats add softness, as does the gathered and ruffled bed skirt. Perfectly pressed white bed linens cozy up to more rustic elements, including the thick woven-jute rug.

OPPOSITE A fresh coat of paint and French lanterns turned this room in a former tractor barn into a perfect spot for a Ping Pong table. ABOVE A pool table and a piano provide more recreation in the adjoining room, which has been dressed up with whitewashed beadboard walls, plush braided-jute floor covering, and a classic Chesterfield sofa upholstered in rustic Belgian linen.

ABOVE In another Hamptons house, boys' and girls' dormitories are tucked upstairs beneath the eaves—a cozy fit for little ones. The boys' room is done in shades of blue. **OPPOSITE** The girls' room is pretty in shades of pink and red. **OVERLEAF** To give this renovated upstate New York farmhouse notes of texture and history, we covered sheet-rock walls with gessoed-and-painted burlap from Elizabeth Dow.

OPPOSITE In an old farmhouse, a stair landing became a home office with the addition of an old trestle table and factory chair. Handkerchief panels at the windows not only allow for privacy but also open to the house's best views. **ABOVE** The Dutch door at the end of a hall hints at the original footprint of the farmhouse. In another case of purposeful transition, adding bookcases and a window seat transformed this hallway into a cheerful library.

ABOVE The zinc-topped bar area allows a bartender to serve from behind the Dutch door. RIGHT In the dining room, washable slipcovers made from old grain sacks dress ultra-comfy upholstered seating intended to keep guests gathered around the table. OVERLEAF LEFT AND RIGHT Rush-seated, Shaker-inspired counter stools make for a friendly breakfast bar and inject a bright, happy pop of red into this New England farmhouse kitchen.

OPPOSITE Linen, oxidized metal, painted-wood furniture, and botanicals are classic country references made fresh with unexpected and earthy color pairings and a contemporary hand-blocked throw pillow. A bedside bouquet of flowers from the garden sweetens this farmhouse bedroom. **ABOVE** A halo of shower curtains converts a footed tub into a shower, and an industrial stool, a wire basket, and a cotton rug dress down the drama. *Three Whales*, a linoleum block print by Linnea Lundmark, nods to the palette.

LUXURIOUSLY MODERN

In general, our preference is toward spaces that are light in spirit, open in vista, and ethereal in perception. And at heart, that is what modern means to us. In our version of modern, the silhouettes are strong. The geometry is precise. The lines are clean. The edges are crisp. There is an overall boldness and graphic clarity to each of the room's elements and to the décor of the room as a whole. We allow, and even welcome, soft moments, sensuous curves, and deluxe details, but they serve as a foil to the otherwise streamlined aesthetic. They are the exceptions that prove the rule, the counterpoints that enhance the experience and excitement of the linearity.

Our modern interiors definitely tip to the contemporary, particularly if we are pulling them together with elements that are primarily new. But when they are eclectic in nature, as so many are, that strong and graphic foundation is preeminent. It grounds the rooms, and with that quiet strength comes the opportunity for variety without any loss of impact. In this way we can incorporate a beloved family heirloom, such as a Chippendale breakfront, into a living room to establish formality. A tall wing chair creates a stylistic bridge with the inherited antique, while simultaneously providing a sculptural silhouette that works toward the modern ends of the mid-century-inspired mix.

We will apply texture on the walls and insert the occasional sculptural moments for contrast or visual relief, but they are design devices. Color, texture, and pattern always factor into how we craft a room's character and style. In so many of our modern rooms, we find that we use palettes that are rich in subtlety and nuance but veer toward the quiet and serene, which suits the simplicity of linear forms. Texture, which the eye may also read as a form of pattern, then comes to the visual fore, but in a subdued manner that adds interest without distraction. This combination of preferences often leads to rooms with an all-encompassing purity that holds true to the tenets of clarity that we see as the foundation of the style.

BECKER

One sure way to make a room feel modern and of the now is to include a piece that is clearly of today. When we take this approach, we do so with those designs that we feel to be classics in the making. As contemporary and on trend as they are, they appear to us to have serious staying power, enough so that we might cautiously deem them the antiques of tomorrow. One such trend that we think has lasting visual value is the natural or cast root and stump pieces that are as much sculpture as they are furniture. There is an inherent timelessness in things organic—they are as they have grown or evolved to be, rather than as we design and make them. Organic elements such as these feel free and daring in an interior. In some way, that may be a contemporary extension of the decorative arts tradition of *faux bois* and *faux marbre*, artful approximations of nature that are long beloved. The modern interpretations of such classic decorative finishes had real chic in years gone by and may now look pleasing to the eye again, thanks to the current revival of interest in the artisanal and pure. Yet every trend has its tipping point, that moment when taste turns, the aesthetic shifts direction again, and modern becomes something altogether new—clean, clear, and instantly classic—once more.

PAGE 121 Crisp geometries read as modern, especially in a glass house such as this. Here we've used square upholstery forms and the triangular travertine coffee tables, which are contemporary and Italian. The luxury comes through materials selection, like the Fortuny fabric on the mid-century Robsjohn-Gibbings chairs, and layering, which includes a patterned area rug over a sisal underpinning. **PRECEDING PAGES** Marrying heirloom and Continental pieces, including the Chippendale breakfront and French clock, with contemporary art and mid-century furniture was one of the most interesting challenges of this project. **LEFT** A double-sided fireplace facing both the living room and the dining area creates a thick floating wall separating the two spaces. It was painted to match the window mullions and ceiling beams to accentuate its architectural importance. **ABOVE** This custom bar cabinet is tucked into the depth of the fireplace partition, but on its opposite wall, facing the windows.

PRECEDING PAGES In the dining area, a table made from reclaimed wood takes center stage. The dark, rich color of the partition fireplace wall shows the art to its best advantage and allows the antique Italian gilded sunburst mirror to shine brilliantly. The floating fireplace provides warmth and focus.
ABOVE AND RIGHT In classic, modern, open-plan style, the dining area flows into the kitchen; utilitarian areas tucked into niches and an island finished to blend with the wood floors further reinforces the visual and spatial connection. The prints on the kitchen counter are by Irving Penn. An American wing chair adds a grace note at the head of the dining table.

LEFT Before a fire that led to a major renovation of this house, we treated the bookcases in the study as part of the wall by painting them the same color, thereby letting the book spines read like patterned wallpaper. Layering artwork in front of the shelving reinforced the look. **ABOVE** When the clients acquired the house, the Parsons table, used here as a desk, was in the kitchen. Native American blankets, layered over sisal, serve as floor covering. **OVERLEAF** In the next iteration of the study, the darker tone of the grasscloth wallcovering and the blackened metal bookcases recede, allowing the objects and the Navajo-inspired carpet by Ralph Lauren to stand out. The Parsons table survived the fire.

ABOVE, CLOCKWISE FROM TOP LEFT To create the feeling of a master suite, we extended the grasscloth wall-covering from the study into the master bedroom, where voluptuous linen drapery panels soften the linear architecture; an Italian folding screen and an Indian textile provide both color and a touch of exoticism; mid-century lamps assert the modern aesthetic; the Maison Baguès–inspired tables and the bullion-fringed sofa add refinement and luxury. OPPOSITE Graphic artwork reinforces the modern vibe.

PRECEDING PAGES In this home on Florida's Gulf shore, Venetian plaster on the ceiling and limestone floors create an elegant backdrop for low-to-the-ground furnishings that keep the spectacular view front and center. A tree-stump coffee table is a purposeful piece of sculpture. ABOVE Strong, clear shapes such as this chair read even stronger when their silhouettes are heightened by the use of color and set against a clean, white backdrop. OPPOSITE The play of textures includes the chairs' cork-covered backs, with figuring that echoes the limestone floors; the hammered, nickel-plated base of the Julian Chichester table; and the cast-bronze, coral-shaped candlesticks.

OPPOSITE In the study, pecky cypress–lined walls create an earthy envelope, setting the tone for a palette of sandy shades drawn from the view and textures that include the sofa's heavy basket-weave linen, inlaid-bone coffee tables, and a rattan desk. **ABOVE** In this vignette, comprising a gilded-driftwood lamp, a hand-carved sideboard, and a quartz crystal–framed mirror, organic meets rustic meets super-refined.

OPPOSITE AND ABOVE In the master bedroom, the saturation of the blues inside matches the intensity of the sun and the blues of the water outside. We wanted the space to be peaceful, so we kept it spare. Diaphanous bed hangings of hand-pieced cotton voile and a grouping of six ethereal flower photographs by artist Rachel Lévy add an airy, romantic touch.

A PARED-DOWN APPROACH

It seems so much a part of human instinct to amass possessions to make a home feel cozy and finished. We love to edit back the belongings, to pare down the possessions to find the right balance. We work to create a certain amount of atmosphere using space, air, movement, and light. Achieving it is a process that happens organically and in layers. At each stage of a project, from conception through installation and after, we focus on getting the visual texture and sensibility right.

Paring down is also our way of modernizing more traditional interiors. Perhaps we came to this approach after an overload of the heavy-handed decorating style of the 1980s, when more was more and the mastery of design and the decorative arts was equated with the ability to incorporate as much ornament and richness as possible. Those rooms could be and often were very beautiful. They were also very formal, serious, and visually dense. We find that traditional rooms done with a light hand may be livable, sophisticated, and friendly. They can be lovely enough for entertaining, and make the clients feel pulled together and grown up, but not as if they are living in their parents' or their grandparents' house. In contrast, the rooms that we call modern or modernist reflect a pared-down approach practically by definition. The discipline of less is more comes naturally into play because it, along with the absence of ornament, provides this style with its philosophical foundation. The luxury comes from the choice of materials and the elegant simplicity of the forms.

There is a constant refinement in how we edit and determine what is right. It does not happen in one fell swoop. We are confident enough to take chances, and to correct them if necessary. We would rather something be plain than distracting. Our urge to pare away may be less an aesthetic choice than an emotional and physical one. Clutter unnerves and unsettles us. That translates into our work. For us, the pared-down interior stems from within: it not only looks right, it has the right tangible sensibility.

OPPOSITE In this classic minimal modern house, clean lines, essential forms, luxurious materials, and an understated palette feel right at home. The Warren Platner coffee table adds a quiet glimmer. **OVERLEAF** The variegated weave of the daybed fabric subtly shifts color over the course of the day and with the seasons. Curtainless windows maximize the view of the woods and make daylight an active element in the room. Underfoot is a hand-knotted custom rug that captures all the variations of grays and silvers used throughout. The club chairs are upholstered in velvet, which contributes another lush texture to the mix.

ABOVE Back-painted glass cabinetry in the kitchen presents a sleek, clean surface uninterrupted by hardware. **OPPOSITE** The dining area bridges the gap between the living room and kitchen; the sinuous shape of the table base echoes the curve of the grand piano. **OVERLEAF** The variations of gray continue in the family room, where natural textures and the tonality of the cowhide rug combine harmoniously. So as not to obscure the view, we kept the sectional seating low and clean lined. **PAGE 152** In the master bedroom, hand-dipped curtain panels introduce an element of softness into the rectilinear environment. **PAGE 153** The bed is upholstered in woven linen of variegated tonalities; carved and painted panels lend surface interest to the wall behind the bed, while a carpet of undyed wool provides plushness underfoot.

A NOD TO TRADITION

In the 1980s the landscape of American decorating celebrated tradition. It was a gilded age. There was delight in lavish layering and extravagant embellishment, and in the inspiration and overlay of historical reference. One of the several types of interior chic prevalent in those days involved an exuberant, knowledgeable, collected eclecticism. Fine antique furniture and luxurious fabrics were very much in vogue in this style, and ornament was everywhere. What we saw and absorbed about this particular type of design in those formative years suggested to us that beautiful rooms coalesce through, and because of, the selection and placement of furnishings and objects that hail from a range of periods and places: French and English, Russian and Swedish, German and Italian, plus, of course, the Asian countries.

Our early introduction to the spirit of the mix still informs the rooms we design today. Though schooled in the classic balance that our decorating predecessors established, we prefer to take liberties with that balance—to recalibrate it for the way we live now. We also range farther afield, as that is the nature of design and decoration today. That said, context is an essential factor in the way we shape our decisions about décor, and so is the vernacular. If we are working on a classic Shingle Style beach house or a country farmhouse in upstate New York, we will create English- and American-inspired interiors because they are appropriate to their environments and true to the local idiom of design. But we will include Continental furniture and mid-century moments to add depth and resonance—and to allude to heritage, travel, and thrift.

Our traditional interiors always include antiques, some more so than others. Antiques are evocative. They add atmosphere, age, and patina to a room. They endow it with an undeniable feeling of the familiar, by which we mean the emotional and visual comfort of forms and materials that are tried, true, and trusted. For that reason, we don't tend to do esoteric

furniture layouts in our more historically inflected projects. In these kinds of interiors, however beautiful they may be, we aim for a subdued sensibility, an air of peace and quiet: we don't want to challenge the eye or tax the mind.

When we nod to history, we nod to it with and through form, pattern, color, and materials. We may emphasize certain wood species that speak to time's passage, and the stone and metalwork that give a patina of age and provide references to bygone eras. We include the plaid and patterned rugs that hint at different times and other places. We select printed fabrics that capture the sensibilities of earlier days through scale and palette. The hues and tones we choose tend to be full of warmth and depth.

So much of our approach to traditional interiors comes via a comparison to what we consider appropriate for more modern spaces. The two are the antithesis of one another—warm, soft, and rounded vs. sharp, bold, and crisp—the opposite ends of the decorating spectrum. Tradition for us is something of a loose fantasy, rather than a tight construct of provenance and period. Since we are free to interpret the forms, textures, colors, patterns, details, and ornamentation that define the different historical styles and the trajectory of American design, we can create rooms that nod, even bow, to tradition with all the comforts of now.

PAGE 155 In a contemporary house designed in the spirit of one of John Russell Pope's nineteenth-century Shingle Style beauties, our concept was to honor tradition but not revere it. PRECEDING PAGES Pride of place in the dining room goes to an American Federal table and Georgian chairs. We paired a voluptuous 1940s Venetian-glass chandelier overhead with an Art Deco mirror over the fireplace, allowing the shocks of cobalt blue to inject modernity into the mix while speaking to the sea in the ship dioramas on display. ABOVE A William Morris pattern inspired the dining room's stenciling by decorative artist Deirdre Newman. OPPOSITE A large passageway leads to the house's central hall, where a table skirted in heavy cotton adds gentle formality; artwork dominates a vestibule to heighten its importance.

ABOVE The owners of this house in the Hamptons collect twentieth-century art that is Long Island born, including works by Perle Fine, Fairfield Porter, and John Little. Over the sofa hangs Perle Fine's arresting canvas *Joie de Vivre* (ca. 1962–63). **OPPOSITE** The large living room has a pair of French doors leading to porches and patios, so curtains help the transition between indoors and out. Another Perle Fine painting hangs between the doors. **OVERLEAF** To create intimate spaces for two or four and comfortable seating for as many as twenty, we established several conversational groups and included plenty of pull-up options, such as the ottoman and occasional chairs, as extra perches. A Fairfield Porter canvas hangs over the fireplace. The mahogany bookcases flanking the fireplace are originally from Harvard University.

LEFT AND ABOVE In a grand entry hall with a sweeping elliptical stair, we kept the furnishings to the elegant essentials to create a breezy passageway and a showcase for the client's remarkable cane collection. Bronze wall sconces designed by Fran Taubman echo the custom bronze stair railing. A large tufted ottoman floats in the room as a graceful catch-all.

PRECEDING PAGES AND ABOVE This paneled library reflects the passions of its owner, who collects first editions of eighteenth- and nineteenth-century travelogues and expedition journals. A 1930s globe suggests the client's orbit. With American Pembroke tables flanking the sofa and an Italian specimen marble–topped table and golden glazed-ceramic lamps, the mix is equally refined and global. Hanging a Perle Fine painting in front of the books adds just a touch of irreverence. **OPPOSITE** The colors of this drop-front Swedish desk are uncharacteristic of the type but perfect for the room, as is a painting by Mary Abbott. **OVERLEAF** Awash in a subtle shade of pale green-gray, the kitchen features a zinc-topped island, custom hood, and range back; soapstone counters; and a backsplash of undulating hand-thrown tiles, which capture all the tones of gray in their crackle glaze.

CHEF DANIEL BOULUD

Summer on a Plate

THE IVY The Restaurant and its Recipes

staffmeals

THE RIVER CAFE COOK BOOK

RIVER CAFE COOK BOOK TWO

KITCHEN SUPPERS

THE DEAN & DELUCA COOKBOOK

AA GILL

PRECEDING PAGES This eat-in kitchen honors the tradition of congregating, with comfortable dining chairs and an adjacent seating area. An oval-shaped English hunt board takes center stage but allows for ease of passage. Crowning the table is a playful craftsman-made zinc chandelier from the 1920s. ABOVE A balcony porthole overlooks the pool house and the beach beyond. OPPOSITE The exterior has several outdoor rooms both adjacent to the house and at poolside. We limited the majority of the furnishings to a suite of teak pieces, which establishes a quiet uniformity that doesn't compete with the plantings and views and will weather naturally along with the shingled exteriors of the house and outbuildings.

OPPOSITE A screened porch runs along the entire east side of the house, outside the living room and library. The challenge for us was to establish distinct areas and intimate moments in that length. In the dining area, a Shaker table and set of chairs seat twelve. Back-to-back antique Bar Harbor–style rattan sofas with lounge chairs form two separate seating groups. Glazed-ceramic garden stools in a basket-weave pattern create a textural play with the actual woven materials. **ABOVE** A second-floor sleeping porch offers a great, cozy place for reposing with a book. The mirror is newly fashioned from salvaged architectural details.

THE POWER OF COLOR

We love color in all its variety, but the degree to which we infuse different hues into a project depends on the client, the location, and the space. In our rooms, color may come from something as simple and transient as an arrangement of flowers. A piece of art may set the tone. In residences where folk furniture feels at home, a painted piece may provide the inspiration or the contrast. For instance, in a bright contemporary room done in shades of blue, layers of contrasting yellow and marigold make for a happy mix. Then a pop of mesmerizing chartreuse—in the form of a painted antique blanket chest doing duty as a coffee table—injects just that diverting note of surprise that enhances every other color in the room and makes the overall composition of colors more personal and appealing. Just by virtue of a fabulous finish, an everyday object may add another work of art to a room—and become a statement piece for that very reason.

Color is the design element most like a musical note. Each note has a definite beauty on its own, but each becomes richer, more resonant, and more memorable when combined with others in a chord. The same holds true for each hue and tonal value we use in a room. Every tinge, tint, or shade affects all the others—those next to it, of course, but also those at a farther remove. Texture and finish come into play. The quality of the light as it changes throughout the day and year has an enormous impact on our color choices. Almost always, the tonal palettes we create for individual rooms evolve when we experience the nature of the daylight at the site. The hues may become more or less saturated based on how they play in the space, respond to the shade of the floor, and reflect the world beyond the windows.

We find that slightest hints of tint can be sufficient to alter an environment. Color is exciting. It is energizing. It can transform a room. It brings vitality to an environment. Life feels too short to live without it.

OPPOSITE For a burst of color and shine in a windowless room, we lacquered the walls in powder blue, matching the cotton velvet on the sofa. Underfoot is a traditional American hooked cotton rug in a contemporary abstract pattern. Also in textural contrast with the glowing walls are the worn painted finishes on the blanket chest and faux-bamboo bench, as well as the thick woven tweed on the pair of Dunbar winged slipper chairs.

ABOVE Perle Fine, *Untitled (No. 56)*, 1950, oil on canvas, © A. E. Artworks, LLC. **OPPOSITE** We often take our color cues from an important piece of art, such as the Perle Fine canvas in this master bedroom. Within a large room that opens onto a sleeping porch, bed hangings define an area of intimacy. **OVERLEAF LEFT AND RIGHT** A Wedgwood vase filled with brilliant yellow ranunculus, a seascape, and blue-trimmed linens dress up a bathroom while contributing to the overall color statement. **PAGES 184–85** In a guest bedroom with a soothing palette of pale yellow-greens and grays, as well as a pleasing symmetry, a mismatched pair of vintage blue-and-white quilts provides a jolt of graphic energy.

PRECEDING PAGES In the sitting room/living room of a contemporary Colonial in Washington, Connecticut, an odd piece of American portraiture that caught the clients' fancy suggested the color palette. Interestingly, these clients are modernists at heart, so we updated their bergères with horizontal stripes and bright orange contrast cord, stripped the sofas bare of trimmings, and joined the seating groups with a classic Parsons coffee table. A contemporary rug woven of jute and leather adds texture on the floor. OPPOSITE AND ABOVE In a subterranean games room, saturated color against bright white millwork and a play of textures create a feeling of warmth and welcome. OVERLEAF Pale blush linen walls and shapely upholstery quiet the overscale geometric pattern of the hooked rug, the bold print of the linen curtains, and the abstract painting by Edith Prellwitz.

ABOVE In a classic blue-and-white breakfast bay overlooking the waterfront on Shelter Island, a polished-marble Saarinen table brightens the grouping. **OPPOSITE** In the formal living room that adjoins the kitchen, an oversize photo of a giant copper beech is centered on the wall. The furnishings are arranged in such a way that the photo becomes part of, not the point of, the decorating.

BOHEMIAN GLAMOUR

Experience has taught us that when it comes to décor, people gravitate naturally to the style that makes them feel most at home. For some, comfort comes in timeless interiors. Others are aware that they are most at ease amid traditional trappings. Still others know they will only be happy in modern rooms. Those styles are very broad, to be sure. But their parameters are quite clear. Bohemian glamour, on the other hand, is highly attuned to a very personal style. In that sense, it is very much about a particular approach to the one-of-a-kind rooms that we favor.

We find bohemian glamour to be very dynamic and exciting. For us, it means using design and decoration in a particularly creative way: that is, expressively, to tell the client's story. In such rooms, each choice comes with additional layers of meaning. Beyond pleasing aesthetics and functional practicalities, the elements of the room must capture a personality and an approach to life—and do so clearly and forcefully, but without shouting.

Almost by definition, rooms that epitomize bohemian glamour are overtly eclectic, full of pattern on pattern, wonderfully colorful, with vivid, arresting, and unusual accents. That said, they are not maximalist per se, and they are not just about more being more. Yet they do overflow with a rich, occasionally eccentric riot of visual information. Our role in such projects is to establish calm amid visual cacophony, to relieve the visual density yet still reveal the personality, because when there is too much to take in, the eye has nowhere to pause or relax. Organic elements, natural textures, and references from far-flung cultures, both ancient and modern, provide the comforts of informality along with textural richness. Material selections are key: from high polish and gilt to the primitive and tribal, the wide array brings the bohemian and the glamour home to the same space.

Interiors in the style that we call bohemian glamour challenge us to establish an unusually delicate balance because they can so easily go over the top. The style itself—and our visually adventurous clients—may afford us an unusual liberty when it comes to layering and collecting. It allows us to explore beauty at random, and of many different kinds. We are mindful to use simplicity as an offset and a complement to the variety because we want the variety to sing. Clean details are quieting. We always go step by step, piece by piece, assessing and editing, adding and subtracting, standing back to consider how the combination of components works in concert—or, in these rooms, en masse.

At first glance, bohemian glamour as we see it clearly includes organic and tribal components and patterns, and restrained touches of opulence here and there. But as we look closer, the elements range far wider than those categories suggest and are certainly more idiosyncratic than is our norm. Every piece has its own unique allure. Somehow, through some form of design intelligence and decorative magic, the components come together to create rooms that feel deeply personal and quite revealing, that have a narrative. The mix works because it is so distinctive and individual, with nothing at all generic. That is what bohemian glamour is really all about.

PAGE 195 In the living room of a small Fifth Avenue apartment, a cast-bronze tree-trunk coffee table, an Eames chair upholstered in a vintage Suzani and patchwork, root-based end tables, and a lacquered-and-walnut custom cabinet from The New Traditionalists make a highly personal statement. **PRECEDING PAGES** The skirted table can and does do double duty for dining when required. The large abstract canvas by Leah Durner was inspired by a Prada fashion show. **ABOVE** As far as placement goes, there's a conscious irreverence in stacking books in front of artworks. **OPPOSITE** Amid all the textiles, an Hermès scarf introduces additional color and pattern.

LEFT AND ABOVE In a room at the back of the apartment without good views, walls glazed in Ralph Lauren's high-impact Poppy Bright Canvas Specialty Finish for depth and color create an inward focus and cleverly conceal all the modern necessities, like HVAC.

OPPOSITE We gave a small breakfast area a glamorous makeover by treating it as another room. Bringing warmth and sophistication are a textured wallcovering from Phillip Jeffries and the inclusion of a high-back leather settee dressed up with a velvet cushion; a faux-animal-print carpet grounds the space with a bit of whimsy. **ABOVE** A vintage table setting with a marbleized glaze dates to the 1970s, while printed-linen napkins and faux-bamboo flatware create a more casual look for everyday use. **OVERLEAF** In the bedroom, a mirror-framed bed and lamb throw speak to glamour. With the bed placed in front of the window, the curtain panels provide the feeling of bed hangings.

THE LOTTERY SHIRLEY JACKSON

ABOVE AND OPPOSITE In 2014 the Kips Bay Decorator Show House took over one of McKim, Mead & White's fabulous Villard houses across from St. Patrick's Cathedral. Much of the original architectural detail survives, including these very formal paneled walls, which we inset with hand-marbleized wallpaper by Calico. We also glazed an arched niche with antique mirror. The bohemian mix incorporates a vintage open-frame brass chair, a 1950s "Calla" torchère, a velvet daybed, and a seductive painting by Natasha Law atop a contemporary carpet from Doris Leslie Blau.

LEFT One of the room's references to nature is this little sculpture of abstracted fiddleheads. **ABOVE** A vintage 1970s "Terra" coffee table by Silas Seandel adds an artisan touch; Seandel cast bronze details into the concrete top in a painterly fashion.

OPPOSITE A silk screen by A.S.V.P. commands attention along one wall; flanking it is a pair of Venini opaline table lamps set symmetrically atop a Grosfeld House mirrored console. **ABOVE, CLOCKWISE FROM TOP LEFT** Giving the eyes a pause from the marbleized pattern is a pair of small paintings by Thomas Libetti; a Pierre Frey metallic woven damask, inspired by the Roaring Twenties, has great, unexpected scale; an agate-topped table injects a natural element into the room, and the base looks like a jewelry setting; a blue Lucite tray colors the reflections in the mirrored top of the console on which it rests.

PRECEDING PAGES This residence in the Printing House, a converted factory space in Greenwich Village, has the grand volumes and open plan that characterize modern-day loft living. For us, that posed the age-old question of how to make a vast space inviting and practical. We used the rug to set the boundaries of the living room area; a curved sofa in the corner directs traffic and facilitates conversation. A play of textures and patterns creates warmth. **OPPOSITE** Familiar upholstery forms such as the Bridgewater sofa help ground the interior and give it a sense of homecoming. **ABOVE** Sculptural lamps and the kitchen counter stools make reference to the building's industrial past.

OPPOSITE Oddly shaped rooms carved out of the existing structure are among the quirks of loft living. The home office has one wall that is double height; it read as a library, so we double-dared it with a photographic trompe l'oeil wallpaper of bookshelves by Tracy Kendall and pulled the room's happy color palette from the "book" covers. TOP The other side of the room is a low, intimate niche with a dropped ceiling, perfect for a bed or settee. ABOVE Dark-painted walls double down on the intimate effect and create an optimal backdrop to showcase the collection of monoprints by Joe Barnes.

ABOVE Ethnic patterns such as this wonderful zigzag print from Osborne & Little bring the touch of the hand—and the faraway—home for chic and stylish clients with a global perspective and a love of fine French antiques. **RIGHT** In a traditional New York loft, old radiators and cast-iron columns speak to history. A pair of bergères gave us an opportunity to be particularly playful with textiles, so we upholstered their exposed backs with a Suzani-inspired print. That fabric just hints at the pattern and colors in the authentic kilim that dresses the ottoman, which acts as an informal coffee table. These tribal textiles serve as counterpoints to the clients' treasured French antiques. Their gilded barometer is hung prominently between the windows and a *bureau plat* is still used as a writing table opposite the sectional.

ABOVE AND OPPOSITE The dining area continues the eclecticism. A collection of engravings hangs above a contemporary Lawson-Fenning sideboard, which is flanked by fauteuils. A set of painted Swedish chairs surrounds the American mid-century dining table. A contemporary gilt-metal étagère placed between the living and dining areas connects the two spaces.

ABOVE AND OPPOSITE In the nursery, the wallpaper from Cole & Son has a charming pattern of vintage hot-air balloons straight from the era of the Montgolfier brothers. A wide-striped cotton rug by Madeline Weinrib and the white contrast cord on the comfortable velvet-covered sofa contribute a graphic crispness, while a sweetly painted fauteuil in its original brocade upholstery adds a delicate, if daring for a nursery, touch.

ABOVE A carved and painted Art Nouveau armoire sets a vintage tone while adding much-needed storage in a Greenwich Village apartment. **RIGHT** Natural materials like linen upholstery, sisal carpet, and dhurrie-covered poufs mix with an industrial coffee table with a reclaimed-wood top and Chinese glazed lamps to toughen the room's more feminine forms, like the skirted sofa, cabriole-legged armchair, and caned-back French-style side chairs. Fashion illustrations, hung gallery style, unify the room. It's a bohemian, eclectic, fashionable mix that still typifies the Village.

FASHION STATEMENTS

We are very fortunate to have a number of leaders in the world of fashion as clients, including Anna Wintour, Jay Fielden, and Jason Wu. It is an understatement to say that each has a strong persona, especially as each plays a significant part in defining the visual landscape that we all survey on a daily basis. This creates an interesting paradigm shift for us as designers. Other clients need our vision to help guide them, but our fashion clients rely on us to fulfill their strong visions. For them, we refine.

It is an exciting process to take on, to live this other persona. On some level, we are hyper-alert, receptors and translators both. We have to be in order to create a decorative language that makes a space personally reflective. With visual people who also happen to be very stylish, that challenge becomes particularly nuanced. And when they possess exceptionally good taste, we are delighted to walk their path.

We often use smaller decorative moments to explain the personality at home and express brand identity in a corporate environment. When Jason Wu wanted to warm up his all-white industrial-chic atelier, we inserted vintage French doors, flannel portiere panels, wallpaper made from the pages of the *New York Observer*, and little pops of color for playfulness. A turned leg on a steel table marries the contemporary to the desired historical reference. The space remains functional. The details speak softly.

For the reception area of *Vogue* in its former offices at 4 Times Square, we took a straightforward approach to palette, scale, and cleanliness. The space is attractive, yet above all it has personality—one that reflects the editorial viewpoint.

Related by visual language, fashion and design are very different. Fashion is about trends. It anticipates what is new and what is next. That is the antithesis of what we do. Our philosophy is based on seeing through the trends to create a timeless, steadfast body of work. We exercise restraint. Like these clients, however, we edit—severely. That is our translation point.

OPPOSITE The *New York Observer* wallpaper produced by Elizabeth Dow is the scene-stealer in Jason Wu's conference room; not only does the pinky peach color warm up these otherwise industrial interiors, but it also flatters the clients. Ochre's Arctic Pear chandelier and Fasem's "Charme" chairs in black metal with tufted-leather seats are glamorous, contemporary moments that counterbalance the raw concrete floors and wood table.

A clean architectural envelope with bright white walls and concrete floors ensures that the clothes stand out. Sales tables with blackened sheet-metal tops and turned legs illustrate Jason's design philosophy of referencing the past to create something new and modern.

The space was once a sweatshop, which just shows the difference a century can make. Vintage nineteenth-century parlor doors salvaged from an estate in Hudson, New York, and painted in Jason's signature shade of gray mark the entrance to the conference room.

ABOVE In the vestibule, artisan-made chairs have caned-metal seats and backs, and cast-metal frames that reinterpret a traditional French form. **OPPOSITE** To warm up the waiting area for Jason's office, we used an irreverent mix of shapely modern chairs, a French-style settee, and an industrial coffee table.

PRECEDING PAGES The challenge here was to transform a commercial lobby into a place of arrival that equals the brand recognition of *Vogue*. We interpreted the client's image and special type of chic into the corporate language. **ABOVE AND OPPOSITE** Anna Wintour's office at *Vogue*'s former headquarters in the heart of Times Square was a stylish respite within the towering commercial center. A refined and fearless combination of patina, modernity, and industry reflects *Vogue*'s brand as defined by its editor in chief.

PERSONAL HISTORIES

Mara and I met in our final semester of the interior design program at the Fashion Institute of Technology. That we both transferred to FIT from elsewhere is serendipitous, to say the least. For me, the youngest of five children raised on a farm in upstate New York, the road to the *AD* 100 was not exactly straight and narrow. Outside the pages of the long-gone Montgomery Ward "Wish Book" mail-order catalogue that I grew up with, the notion of interior decoration was not given much consideration in my home then, and it still proves to be a challenging topic for my parents today. Chairs were meant to be comfortable, carpets low maintenance (that is, hide dirt and pet hair), curtains for privacy, and lights, well . . . you guessed it! Perhaps it was my parents' indifference toward design that encouraged me. At least they never objected to my occasional rearrangement of the living room furniture.

I grew up in an old farmhouse on the edge of town. Like many Victorian-era farmhouses in that area, it had good bones, even when it showed its age. I loved living in an old place and appreciated its elegant enfilade of rooms, high ceilings, and tall windows. In my part of central New York, the landscape is a bit reminiscent of the Midwest—lots and lots of open space, punctuated by barns and outbuildings. Those buildings were authentic and true to the American farm vernacular, with a simplicity of structure and a focus on function that I still find very appealing.

In school, art class was an outlet for me, really the only period of the day that seemed too short. In middle school, I was invited to participate in creating a mural for the school cafeteria (which still exists!). The theme was the Erie Canal, which runs through my hometown. As the one farmer in the group, my contribution, naturally, was illustrating the mule pulling a barge. This, in addition to working on subsequent school murals and set designs for school plays, serving as the yearbook photographer, and a few side jobs painting signs for local businesses, garnered me the title of "most creative" in my high school yearbook.

Mara's cousin the photographer Sam Frost took our portrait in the reception area of our office, where a nineteenth-century Regency sofa upholstered in hemp and decorated with throw pillows covered in a Carolina Irving fabric is an invitation to sit. John Tipton's long, dynamic artwork combining photography and text provides both a graphic punch and a soulful note.

My middle school mural (circa 1985)—an early example of artistic license!

However gratifying that title may have been, it instilled a bit of panic in me, for my path seemed far less clear than I imagined it was for those crowned "best athlete" or "most likely to succeed." Where was I to go from here? At the recommendation of my school guidance counselor, the local Rotary Club sponsored me as a foreign exchange student for the summer following graduation.

The experience was life-altering. I was hosted by a family in the northeast corner of France, on the border of Luxembourg. The family ran a small boutique in their eighteenth-century village and owned an elegant home on one of its windy, cobblestone streets. I was truly charmed by their lifestyle and the history and culture of their surroundings—a foreign exchange in every sense for me.

That fall, quite by default, I began my freshman year as a fine arts major at a liberal arts college in upstate New York. To me, with my eyes wide open and the taste of French wine still fresh on my lips, the prospect seemed bleak, and the farmer in me knew how impractical (or impossible) a career in fine arts might be. Though my classes in art history, painting, and drawing were enjoyable, I knew by second semester that I had to change course. One short year post-Paris, I found myself on Amtrak, New York City bound.

———

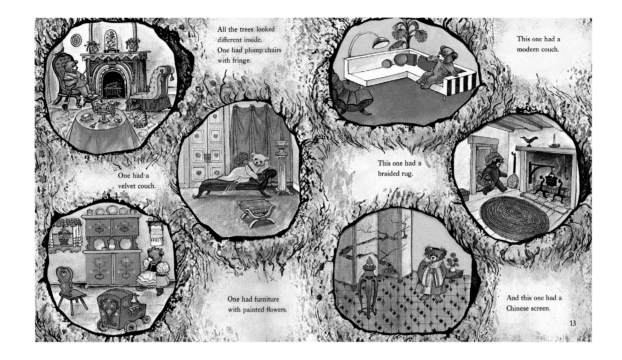

Evelyn Scott's *The Fourteen Bears: Summer and Winter*, illustrated by Virginia Parsons, was my childhood favorite. Though Henrietta's color-blocked International Style room was striking, I was more smitten with the bear striking a pose on her Biedermeier recamier.

My trajectory toward interior design seems much more natural than Jesse's. I grew up in a Hudson River Valley suburb of New York City. My parents were schoolteachers whose love of history translated into family vacations with educational and historical components. My favorite book as a child, *The Fourteen Bears: Summer and Winter*, introduced me to the idea of design and the decorative arts. The book is a charmingly illustrated story that peeks into each bear's home, every one of which has its own distinct historical style—Colonial, Bavarian, Swedish, Renaissance, and so on. There was even an International Style bear: her name was Henrietta, and she had round glasses. I spent hours studying all the pictures of interiors and matching up the bears with their bedrooms and living rooms, summer and winter.

Since early childhood, I've had a deep love of old homes, museums, and historical landmarks, and especially of rustic things. Because we lived in an area rich in historical sites and house museums, parental and school trips to these treasures were the norm. While I no longer remember the historical significance of most of those places, I clearly recall the patterned gardens I first saw in Colonial Williamsburg, the dizzying patterns of carpets at Boscobel, the lime-plastered stone walls of a kitchen in Philipsburg Manor, the creak and slant of wide-plank flooring, and the smell of an old home penetrated by wood smoke. I found the world of these houses so much more beautiful and intriguing than my family's modest ranch home.

While my home life was certainly neither grand nor particularly artistic, my family has produced several generations of artists—Michele Oka Doner and Sam Gross are distant cousins, along with other working artists and antiques dealers. I guess an artistic bent was in the genes, and I always drew. I used to draw floor plans all the time. If I liked a house, I drew up its floor plan—and I still do—to remember it better.

As I got older, I found practical ways to think about homes. I began poring over the *New York Times* Real Estate section and watching renovation programs such as *This Old House*. A friend's father with a design-and-build company liked that I had an interest in construction, and he would explain floor plans and take me on site visits. That inspired me to take drafting classes in high school (I was the only girl in this trade program!). Instead of doing

In 2011 we represented *Town & Country* in Hearst's Designer Visions Showhouse, unique among show houses in that it assigns participating design firms an entire apartment to decorate rather than a single room. *Town & Country*, being more lifestyle than shelter oriented, offered to do a story on the apartment in the January 2012 issue that featured us both as designers and as a family. We usually style our rooms for shoots, so it was exciting to work with fashion stylists who paired our clothing and looks to the interiors that we had designed.

a preprofessional major in college, I chose art history with a minor in fine arts. It was there that I began to realize how natural visual learning was for me—and that it was a powerful way of communicating. I understood the nature of a line and how emotion or energy could be expressed through something that simple. Through my art history classes I learned how the eye could be controlled by composition, and that all styles and mediums were informative and expressive. For the first time I believed that art was not frivolous and self-indulgent, but serious and important (or at least very interesting) in the way it defined and influenced society. That epiphany emboldened me to transfer to FIT to pursue interior design, a field that combined all my loves and fascinations.

———————

At FIT, the interior design program split each class into two parallel groups of students. For the first three years, Mara and I were in different groups and didn't really know each other. In my first two years there, I found the program interesting, but what was most exciting was the opportunity that the city had to offer. In contrast to the rural places I had lived, I couldn't believe how much was at my fingertips—simply posted on the school's job board! At first I assisted an interior photographer and learned what a patient and precise craft it is to capture the atmosphere of an empty room. Then I worked as a freelance photographer for a location agency. The agency would send me out to different locations, usually residences, to take scouting shots for its catalogues. Seeing the interiors of those extraordinary homes was a fantastic education. Occasionally I would see a home I had scouted published in a magazine and discover it was the work of a notable designer. That immersion was thrilling. Having actually been in those homes made the theory we were learning in the studio come to life. I switched into Mara's group in our senior year to accommodate an internship with Thomas O'Brien at Aero Studios.

———————

Like Jesse, I, too, was determined to get as much industry experience as I could while still a student. My first internship was at *Modern Bride* magazine, which had just expanded its home design department. The many different looks the editors produced issue after issue exposed me to an enormous spectrum of styles and to so many objects and furnishings—salt cellars, knife rests, Welsh cupboards—that had not been a part of my upbringing. It was also an introduction to stylists, photographers, and the furniture and tabletop markets—and to how hardworking the editorial world was. While in college I also worked in M. A. Jackson's interiors shop, housed in a converted barn in Cross River, New York, and in K. M. Antiques of London, a shop specializing in English accessories in New York's Decoration and Design Building. I spent my senior year in the interiors department at Ike & Kligerman Architects, which offered me my first job upon graduation.

———

As we mentioned in the Introduction, after we graduated our careers took parallel paths working for renowned designers specializing in residential interiors. Our varied influences have shaped how each of us sees, and what criteria we each factor into our design decisions. Our instincts may be different. And on occasion we'll disagree. Our decision-making process is the dialogue and the dialectic of our relationship—the constant back and forth pushes us to continual refinement.

Experience has taught us that in design, and in life, we are better, stronger, and more insightful as partners. We have learned to look and seek and discover. And perhaps it is this combination of self-knowledge and shared experiences that make us so committed as we continue to build and grow and define ourselves through—and because of—the design firm we've created together: Carrier and Company.

This book is dedicated with love and gratitude to our children, Jack and Natalie,
who have endured not only the growth of our business but all of those "family trips"
to flea markets, antiques shops, and job sites without complaint.

ACKNOWLEDGMENTS

First and foremost, we need to thank our families for their enduring support, even when we pursued paths that were unclear, uncomfortable, or unfamiliar. We also must particularly thank our mothers, Katherine Carrier and Mary Miller, whose "on-demand" babysitting has allowed us to grow a company at the same time we are growing a family.

This book is only possible because of the many wonderful clients who have entrusted us with their homes and businesses. It is a true honor and blessing to work for and with them, and we are grateful to them for allowing us to share their homes with the world.

We must give very special thanks to Anna Wintour and Jay Fielden, our editorial clients, for their encouragement and support. It is their important and far-reaching influence that we credit for our company's success. We are also particularly grateful to Anna Wintour for so graciously agreeing to contribute the foreword to this book.

The support we've received from the design press since we first opened our doors has been humbling, and we cannot thank you enough for your interest in our work and the generous way that you have presented us in your publications. We are grateful to, in alphabetical order: Michael Boodro, Jenny Bradley, Howard Christian, Sophie Donelson, Irene Edwards, Carolyn Englefield, Wendy Goodman, Jason Kontos, Robert Leleux, Ann Omvig Maine, Rebecca Morse, Sabine Rothman, Robert Rufino, Margaret Russell, Clinton Smith, Doretta Sperduto, Newell Turner, and Pilar Viladas.

Our introduction to Mark Magowan at Vendome Press came just as we were beginning to consider the idea of a book, so it seemed a very good omen. The experience that followed—working so intimately with Mark, Jacqueline Decter, Celia Fuller, Irene Convey, and Jim Spivey—has been irreplaceable. The team at Vendome supported our whims and tempered them with elegance and good judgment. Our greatest hope for this book was that it would feel like a projection of our personalities and aesthetic, not just showcase our portfolio. We are so pleased that it does. That only happened because of the patience, careful editing, and personal investment that the Vendome Press team took with it. To be in such caring hands has been a comfort and a blessing.

Jill Cohen was invaluable in helping us find our voice and our vision. Sometimes it is hard to see the forest for the trees, and Jill was able to see us clearly. She opened our eyes to the value in telling our story. Her cheerleading and leadership have guided this book and elevated it from a narrative about design to our narrative about design. More importantly, her astute observations helped us to see our work in a new light and understand that what we do is special.

Judith Nasatir perhaps deserves the most thanks. She spent hours asking us questions and having to listen to (and record) our answers. Her ability to piece together our stream of consciousness into a cohesive and eloquent text was close to miraculous. We often get to work with visual people, doing visual things, and to watch and learn how Judith listened and then was able to produce the very best from us has been a lesson in editing and understanding. Now she knows us better than we know ourselves.

It takes a village to read, edit, review, and critique a book, so there are more thanks necessary. We are grateful to Simon Jutras for his unerring eye and skilled hands in the graphic design and layouts of our photography and portfolio. And we so appreciate the help of Karee Hanifan Auth in organizing the business of the book and keeping us on track with our branding and point of view. Matthew Snyder of Place New York Public Relations has always aided us at pivotal junctures in our business, and we have come to rely on his guidance and savvy.

To the photographers who have captured our work and trained us in styling and "seeing," we are indebted. Thank you Christopher Baker, Eric Boman, Robert Brantley, Chris Cooper, Zach DeSart, Pieter Estersohn, Douglas Friedman, Sam Frost, Nick Johnson, Benjamin Kaufmann, Francesco Lagnese, Peter Margonelli, Eric Piasecki, Marco Ricca, Trevor Tondro, and William Waldron.

A very special thanks to Annie Leibovitz for a once-in-a-lifetime experience of sitting for a family portrait as part of the Corcoran Company's "Live Who You Are" campaign, and then gifting us the image for use in the book. For her to know how we actually live as a family in a cramped New York apartment, and to understand our aesthetic and then entrust us with her home was a professional high.

We would also like to thank our industry colleagues, mentors, peers, and friends, for the support they have shown in so many ways: Sara Bengur, Jeffrey Bilhuber, Nancy Boszhardt, Miranda Brooks, Mario Buatta, Charles Cohen, Ellie Cullman, Jamie Drake, Jim Druckman, Thom Filicia, Alexa Hampton, Ed Hollander, James Huniford, John Ike, Debra Kanabis, Celerie Kemble, Tom Kligerman, Alix Lerman, William Li, Marcy Masterson, Thomas O'Brien, Peter Pennoyer, John David Rose, Tom Scheerer, Stephen Sills, Matthew Patrick Smyth, and Bunny Williams.

And last but not least, heartfelt thanks go to the employees of Carrier and Company for their hard work and commitment to delighting clients, completing jobs, and growing our company over the years: Nicole Adams, Aaron Boehlert, Alisha Pither Greenbaum, Abby Harding, Emily Cappe Innerkofler, Doria Kalt, Molly Kurzweil, Janet Mui, Merrill Peress, Laurie Scovotti, Jeanne Stahlman, and Laura Stanley Tuttle.

SOURCES

ANTIQUES AND FURNITURE

Bernd Goeckler Antiques
bgoecklerantiques.com

BK Antiques
bkantiques.com

Christie's
christies.com

David Duncan Antiques
davidduncanantiques.com

Dering Hall, LLC
deringhall.com

Doyle New York
doylenewyork.com

Gary R. Sullivan Antiques
garysullivanantiques.com

Jefferson West
jeffersonwest.com

Jeffrey-Marie Antiques
West Palm Beach, FL
(561) 832-6505

John Rosselli Antiques
johnrosselliantiques.com

John Salibello
johnsalibello.com

Laurin Copen Antiques
laurincopenantiques.com

Liz O'Brien
lizobrien.com

Maison Gerard
maisongerard.com

Sotheby's
sothebys.com

Time and Materials
timeandmaterialsantiques.com

ARCHITECTS

Ampersand, Architecture
ampersandarchitecture.com

David Bae Architect
davidbae.net

Halard-Halard Architecture
& Design
halard-halard.com

Giancarlo Valle
giancarlovalle.com

Gordon Khan Associates
gkassociates.com

John David Rose Architect
johndavidrosearchitect.com

Peter Pennoyer Architects
ppapc.com

Robert Dean Architects
robertdeanarchitects.com

Specht Harpman Architects
spechtharpman.com

Tracy Salladay Architecture PC
salladayarchitect.com

Workshop/APD
workshopapd.com

BUILDERS AND CONTRACTORS

Fanuka
fanuka.com

I. Grace Company
igrace.com

Ironwood Construction
ironwoodconst.com

John Follini
Master Builder
Patchogue, NY

Profile Group
profilegc.com

Silverlining Interiors
silverlininginteriors.com

Taconic Builders
taconicbuilders.com

CARPETS AND RUGS

Beauvais
beauvaiscarpets.com

Crosby Street Studios
crosbystreetstudios.com

Doris Leslie Blau
dorisleslieblau.com

Mitchell Denburg Collection
mitchelldenburg.com

The New England Collection
thenewenglandcollection.com

Sacco Carpet
saccocarpet.com

Stark
starkcarpet.com

Studio Four NYC
studiofournyc.com

Turabian & Sariyan
turabianandsariyan.com

Woodard & Greenstein
woodardweave.com

CUSTOM UPHOLSTERY AND WINDOW TREATMENTS

Dmitriy & Co.
dmitriyco.com

H&R Drapery
hr-drapery.com

Luther Quintana
lqupholstery.com

Naples Custom Designs
& Upholstery
ncdandu.com

Naula
naulaworkshop.com

New York Drapery
nydinc.com

The Recovery Room
New Milford, CT
(860) 350-6244

DECORATIVE PAINTERS

Deirdre Newman
deirdrenewman.com

Phillip Bland
pb-deco.com

Toby Nuttall
tobynuttall.com

FABRICS AND TRIMS

Bennison Fabrics
bennisonfabrics.com

Brunschwig & Fils
brunschwig.com

Carolina Irving Textiles
carolinairvingtextiles.com

Chapas Textiles
chapastextiles.com

Chelsea Textiles
chelseatextiles.com

Claremont
claremontfurnishing.com

Cowtan & Tout
cowtan.com

Edelman Leather
edelmanleather.com

Holland & Sherry
interiors.hollandandsherry.com

John Rosselli & Associates
johnrosselli.com

Kravet
kravet.com

Lee Jofa
leejofa.com

Osborne & Little
osborneandlittle.com

Pierre Frey
pierrefrey.com

Quadrille
quadrillefabrics.com

Schumacher
fschumacher.com

GALLERIES, ART CONSULTANTS, AND FINE ART FRAMERS/ INSTALLERS

Berry Campbell
berrycampbell.com

Elizabeth Sadoff Art Advisory
esadoff.com

Gallery of Graphic Arts Ltd.
galleryofgraphicartsnyc.com

ILevel Art Placement
& Installation
ilevel.biz

Stephanie Hoppen Gallery
stephaniehoppen.com

Voltz Clarke
voltzclarke.com

HARDWARE

The Nanz Company
nanz.com

Urban Archaeology
urbanarchaeology.com

Waterworks
waterworks.com

HOME DESIGN STORES

ABC Carpet & Home
abchome.com

Aero Studios
aerostudios.com

Anthopologie
anthropologie.com

English Country Antiques
ecantiques.com

Garden District
gardendistrictnaples.com

Hollyhock
hollyhockinc.com

Jayson Home
jaysonhome.com

John Derian Company
johnderian.com

Mecox
mecox.com

Mitchell Gold + Bob Williams
MGBWhome.com

Ralph Lauren Home
ralphlaurenhome.com

Restoration Hardware
restorationhardware.com

Treillage
treillageny.com

LANDSCAPE ARCHITECTS AND DESIGNERS

Ann Brooke Landscape Design
annbrookedesign.com

Goetz & Strope Landscape
Architects
gsnaples.com

Edmund Hollander Landscape
Architects
hollanderdesign.com

Miranda Brooks Landscape Design
mirandabrooks.com

LIGHTING

Blanche P. Field
blanchefield.com

Circa Lighting
circalighting.com

Rejuvenation
rejuvenation.com

Remains Lighting
remains.com

The Urban Electric Co.
urbanelectricco.com

Vaughan
vaughandesigns.com

RESTORATION AND CUSTOM WORKROOMS

Alliance Restoration
New York, NY
(212) 831-7908

Carlton House Restoration
carltonhouse.net

Costello Studio
csidesigns.net

Falotico Studios
faloticostudios.com

Fran Taubman
Shelter Island, NY
(631) 749-0275

Furniture Place
nyfurnitureshop.com

Sheelin Wilson Gilding Studio
sheelinwilson.com

WALL COVERINGS

The Alpha Workshops
alphaworkshops.org

Gracie
graciestudio.com

Phillip Jeffries
phillipjeffries.com

SJW Studios
sjwstudios.com

First published in the United States of America by
The Vendome Press
1334 York Avenue
New York, NY 10021
www.vendomepress.com

ISBN 978-0-86565-320-7

Editor: Jacqueline Decter
Production Coordinator: Jim Spivey
Designer: Celia Fuller

Library of Congress Cataloging-in-Publication Data
Carrier, Jesse, author.
    Carrier and Company : positively chic interiors / Jesse
Carrier and Mara Miller ; with Judith Nasatir ; Foreword
by Anna Wintour.
        pages cm
    ISBN 978-0-86565-320-7 (hardback)
    1. Carrier and Company. 2. Interior decoration--United
States--Themes, motives. I. Title.
    NK2004.3.C37C37 2015
    747--dc23
                                                    2015025623

This book was produced using acid-free paper, processed
chlorine free, and printed with soy-based inks.

Printed in China by OGI
Second printing

PAGE 1 The high-contrast coupling of the black botanicals by contemporary artist Hugo Guinness with eighteenth-century pieces by Mrs. Delaney creates excitement and glamour in a country house entry. PAGES 2-3 In a glass house where rectilinear forms dominate, the classic shape of a wing chair becomes modern and sculptural. PAGES 4-5 Vintage wicker seating and a Shaker table and chairs nod to tradition on this screened porch. PAGE 6 Hanging an oversize painting by Hugo Guinness above a diminutive Swedish chest of drawers is a play on scale that accentuates the contemporary nature of the artwork in this country house. PAGES 8-9 An up-to-date take on a classic blue-and-white palette freshens a Southampton getaway. PAGE 10 In Anna Wintour's former Times Square office, a chic, knowing blend of periods and styles expresses the *Vogue* brand as defined by its editor in chief.

PHOTO CREDITS

Christopher Baker: pp. 1, 8-9, 26-33, 102, 104-7; Eric Boman: pp. 18-19, 24-25, 97-100; Robert Brantley: pp. 40-43, 45-47, 50-52, 54-57, 62-64; Jesse Carrier: pp. 6, 10, 17, 20-23, 85-97, 101, 186-87, 230 left, 232-35, 238; Chris Cooper: pp. 76-77; Zach DeSart: pp. 2-3, 122-23, 126-29, 132-33, 134 top left, 134 top right, 135, 192-93; Pieter Estersohn: pp. 4-5, 34, 108-9, 155-59, 161-68, 170-71, 174-78, 181, 184-85, 212-13; Douglas Friedman: pp. 224-25; Sam Frost: pp. 14-15, 237; Nick Johnson: pp. 188-89; Ben Kaufman: p. 229; Francesco Lagnese: pp. 110-19, 182-83, 195-205, 240-41; Annie Leibovitz: p. 13; Peter Margonelli: pp. 36-37, 160, 169, 172-73, 190-91, 214-17; Eric Piasecki: pp. 42 left, 48-49, 54 left, 58-61, 65-75, 78-83, 136-44, 146-53, 218-23; Marco Ricca: pp. 206-211; Trevor Tondro: pp. 121, 124-25, 128 left, 134 bottom left, 134 bottom right; William Waldron: pp. 38, 39, 130-31, 226, 228, 230-31